This

The Wildlife Trusts Guide to

# WILD
# FLOWERS

The Wildlife Trusts Guide to

# WILD
# FLOWERS

## Series Editor Nicholas Hammond

Illustrated by Bridgette James

NEW HOLLAND

First published in 2002 by
New Holland Publishers (UK) Ltd
London • Cape Town • Sydney • Auckland

10 9 8 7 6 5 4 3 2 1

Garfield House, 86–88 Edgware Road, London
W2 2EA, United Kingdom
Website: www.newhollandpublishers.com
80 McKenzie Street, Cape Town 8001, South Africa
Level 1/Unit 4, 14 Aquatic Drive, Frenchs Forest,
NSW 2086, Australia
218 Lake Road, Northcote, Auckland, New Zealand

ISBN 1 85974 966 6

Publishing Manager: Jo Hemmings
Project Editor: Mike Unwin/Camilla MacWhannell
Production: Joan Woodroffe

**Packaged by Wildlife Art Ltd:**
www.wildlife-art.co.uk
Design and Cover Design: Sarah Crouch
Art/Copy Editor: Sarah Whittley
Text: Paul Sterry
Proof-reading and Index: Rachel Lockwood
**Illustrator: Bridgette James**

Reproduction by Modern Age
Repro Co. Ltd, Hong Kong
Printed and bound in Singapore by
Kyodo Printing Co (Singapore) Pte Ltd

# Contents

Since 1912, The Wildlife Trusts have been speaking out for wildlife and undertaking practical action at the local level throughout the UK. Believing that wildlife is essential to a healthy environment for all, The Wildlife Trusts work with people from all walks of life – communities, industry, government, landowners, and families – to make sure nature gets a chance amongst all of the pressures of the modern world.

With years of experience and the service of the UK's top naturalists, The Wildlife Trusts and Wildlife Watch – the UK's leading club for young environmentalists – play a key part in restoring the balance between new developments and the natural world. With the specialist skills of volunteers and staff they manage more than 2,300 wildlife reserves (totalling more than 80,000 hectares), which are among the finest sites in the UK.

Their members, who number more than 340,000, contribute to their achievements by their generosity and hard work, and by spreading the message to everyone that wildlife matters.

The Wildlife Trusts is a registered charity (number 207238). For membership, and other details, please phone The Wildlife Trusts on 0870 0367711 or log on to www.wildlifetrusts.org

**M**eadows ablaze with wild flowers in bloom are the romantic ideal for many lovers of the countryside. Of course, when agriculture was less intensive, arable weeds thrived, roadsides had a more varied flora and "unimproved" pasture did have a wonderful variety of flowering plants. There is no doubt that there have been huge losses of habitat for wildlife, but as the last century drew to a close, prospects for wild flowers had begun to improve. Conservationists, such as the 46 Wildlife Trusts, began to draw the attention of land-users to the importance of biodiversity. To their credit local authorities and farmers have begun to take action. The challenge is to continue this restoration of the countryside beyond the confines of nature reserves, where The Wildlife Trusts maintain grazing and hay-cutting regimes to maximise the production of wild flowers.

## Life cycle of flowering plants

The flower is just one part of the life of a flowering plant. The cycle begins with the seed, is followed by the seedling and then grows to the point where it flowers and then fruits to release the seeds that start the cycle again. There are a huge variety of sizes of seeds. Some seeds can survive for many years, lying dormant in the soil, while others are so short-lived they must germinate quickly. Each plant may be able to produce a huge number of seeds, but few will germinate and even fewer will survive to flower. At every stage of its life a plant is vulnerable to predation, weather conditions and accidental destruction.

The roots of seedlings begin to develop before the leaves. Flowering plants are classified into two major orders depending on how the leaves of the seedlings develop. Monocotyledons have one seed leaf or *cotyledons*, while the dicotyledons have two. Once the cotyledons have performed their function of protecting and nourishing the developing seedling, they wither to be replaced by true leaves. Secondary roots develop from the young plant's main roots to create an intricate network probing the soil for the moisture and nutrients. Energy from sunlight is synthesised by chlorophyll, the green pigment in leaves, into carbohydrates, cellulose and starch, by a complex process involving water and carbon dioxide from the air. Growth throughout the plant requires the starches created in the leaves.

It is only when the plant is large enough that it will flower. The flowering stage may be at a specific time so it can take advantage of factors that aid pollination.

Typically the flower consists of sepals, which form a calyx, within which are the petals. Sometimes both sepals and petals are similar and then together are called the *perianth*. Within the petals and sepals are the pollen-producing *stamens*, the male parts of the flowers. The female parts of the flower are the *ovaries*, each with one or more pollen-receptive stigmas often borne on a stalk-like part called a *style*. Seeds develop in the fertilised ovary, which ripens and turns into fruit. This can be juicy and berry-like, or dry.

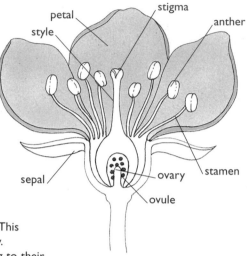

Plants are described according to their flowering and fruiting habits. The shortest-living are the annuals, which complete their lives within a single year and then die. Biennials germinate in their first year, survive through the winter and in their second year flower, seed and die. Perennials flower from year to year, surviving the winter either above or below the ground.

## Leaf types

Typically the structure of a leaf is a stalk with a wide blade on either side of it. The blade is usually flat and may be simple or compound, consisting of several separate leaflets. The variations in leaf shape help in identification, especially when the plant is not flowering. The way in which the leaves are arranged along the stem of the plant varies. Opposite leaves grow from the stem opposite each other, while alternate leaves grow from the opposite side of the stem, but not opposite each other. More than two leaves growing from the same point on the stem are described as *whorled*. Simple leaves are found in a large number of shapes including narrow-elliptical, broad-elliptical, narrow-lanceolate, kidney-shaped, arrow-shaped, and ovate. Compound leaves consist of two or more separate leaflets. Pinnate leaves grow opposite each other, while trifoliate grow in groups of three.

## Flower forms and type

Regular flowers have similar petals and, even when there is an odd number, they give a regular appearance. Irregular flowers are those that are symmetrical only in that each side are similar. Some stems bear single flowers; these are known as solitary. Some flowers appear on spikes of several unstalked flowers on the stem. Clearly stalked individual flowers growing as on a spike are called *racemes*, an example of which is the lady's smock. When each branch of the flower ends in a flower it is a *cyme* such as water forget-me-not. *Umbels* are either flat-topped or domed flowerheads arising from the stem at the same place like an umbrella: this is typical of members of the carrot family such as cow parsley and hemlock.

## Adapting to their environment

Where a plant grows is the first clue to its identity. Some species can thrive in a variety of habitats, while others are restricted. There are several factors that create habitats for plants: rainfall, temperature, soil types and proximity to the sea. Coasts are often exposed to wind and salt spray, but there may be very little fresh water, which means that the plants that survive must have the ability to retain moisture in their thick leaves and cope with salt. Wet habitats produce some spectacular flowering plants. Aquatic plants grow in the water. The flowers of common water-crowfoot float on the surface, while those of arrowhead protrude above the surface of the water. In the acidic peat bogs the plant community includes the broad-leaved sundew, an insectivore that traps and absorbs small insects. Open habitats cover heathland and grassland. Heathland's main characteristics are acidic soils where woodlands were cleared many years ago by man. The upland heaths are known as moorland. Grassland includes arable farmland, acid grassland and calcareous grassland. Intensive agriculture means that arable is dominated by cereal crops, but some arable weeds can survive, especially with the aid of conservation-friendly farming. Acid grassland has a different flora from grasslands on chalk and limestone. Ancient meadows that have not been "improved" have a wealth of flowers. The hedges that border meadows have their own communities of plants. Broad-leaved woodlands contain mature trees and distinct layers of shrub and ground flora.

The 125 species in this book are a very small selection of the northern European list of almost 2000. We have chosen those that are widespread, common and particularly beautiful.

## Hop
*Humulus lupulus*

SIZE AND DESCRIPTION  Up to 6 m tall. A twining, climbing plant that uses other species for support. Stems are square in cross-section, covered in stiff hairs and twine clockwise. Rough-textured palmate leaves are divided into three to five leaflets. Male and female flowers are borne on separate plants. Male flowers are carried in branched clusters. Female flowers are the familiar pendant cone-like hops, green at first but ripening brown.

FLOWERING TIME  August–September.

DISTRIBUTION  Widespread throughout lowland Europe.

HABITAT  Common in hedgerows and scrub habitats; also widely cultivated.

## Mistletoe
*Viscum album*

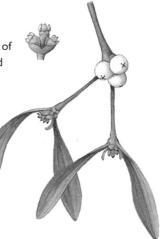

SIZE AND DESCRIPTION  Up to 1 m in diameter.
A woody, perennial parasite found on the branches of
mature, usually deciduous trees, especially apple and
poplars. Forms spherical clumps. Branches evenly
forked. Leaves are oval, leathery and yellowish, and
borne in opposite pairs. Flowers are tiny and
green with four, minute petals; male and female
flowers on separate plants. Berries are white
and sticky and dispersed by birds.
FLOWERING TIME  November–February.
DISTRIBUTION  Widespread throughout central
and southern Europe, avoiding upland areas.
HABITAT  Associated with areas of open woodland
where host tree species flourish.

## Common nettle
*Urtica dioica*

SIZE AND DESCRIPTION  Up to 150 cm tall. An
upright, coarse perennial that is covered with
stinging hairs and which has tough yellowish
roots. Stems are four-angled and bear pairs of
opposite leaves that are ovate and toothed. Flowers
are small, comprising four greenish petals, and are
borne in pendant axillary spikes; male and female
flowers on separate plants. In suitable locations,
it forms extensive patches.
FLOWERING TIME  June–August.
DISTRIBUTION  Widespread throughout
lowland Europe.
HABITAT  Hedgerows, woodlands and
disturbed ground near habitation. Thrives
best on nitrogen-enriched soils.

### Redshank
*Persicaria maculosa*
SIZE AND DESCRIPTION  Up to 80 cm tall. An upright or sprawling annual with red-tinged and much-branched stems. Leaves are narrow, oval and hairless. Sometimes tinged red and invariably showing a dark central spot or smudge. Basal sheath of the leaf has a hairy margin. Pinkish-red flowers are borne in dense axillary and terminal spikes.
FLOWERING TIME  May–October.
DISTRIBUTION  Widespread in lowland central and western Europe.
HABITAT  Favours disturbed, damp soils on cultivated and disturbed ground. Often found at the marshy margins of shallow lakes.

### Common sorrel
*Rumex acetosa*
SIZE AND DESCRIPTION  Up to 60 cm tall. An upright perennial. Leaves are dark green and shaped like an arrowhead; the lower ones are stalked while the upper ones are stalkless and clasp the stem. Leaves taste of vinegar. Flowers are reddish and borne in upright slender spikes. Occasionally, the whole plant may be tinged red.
FLOWERING TIME  May–July.
DISTRIBUTION  Widespread and common throughout much of Europe except for the far south.
HABITAT  Favours a wide range of grassy habitats, from meadows and woodland rides to coastal cliffs and dunes.

## Water dock
*Rumex hydrolapathum*

SIZE AND DESCRIPTION
Up to 2 m tall. A much-
branched perennial, which is
strikingly tall and imposing.
Leaves are 80 cm or more,
tapering at the base and tip; they are
tough and narrow-oval in outline.
Reddish flowers are triangular or heart-
shaped in outline; borne in tight whorls on
upright flowering spikes.

FLOWERING TIME July–September.

DISTRIBUTION Locally common in suitable habitats throughout lowland Europe.

HABITAT Always found in wetland habitats, typically growing beside rivers
and lakes, and sometimes rooted in shallow, muddy water margins.

### Broad-leaved dock
*Rumex obtusifolius*

Size and description Up to 1 m tall. A robust and upright perennial. Stalked leaves are broadly oval, heart-shaped at the base, and 20 cm or more; veins on underside of leaves are hairy. Flowers are small and greenish and borne in whorls along upright flower spikes; these spikes are leafy at the base.

Flowering time June–October.

Distribution Widespread and often abundant in suitable habitats throughout lowland Europe.

Habitat Favours disturbed ground such as field margins, tracks and waste ground.

### Good-King-Henry
*Chenopodium bonus-henricus*

Size and description Up to 50 cm tall. An upright perennial. Typically greenish but sometimes tinged red. Leaves are up to 10 cm long and triangular, the lower ones most noticeably so; leaf surface is mealy when young but becomes smooth and green with age. Stems sometimes show red lines. Flowers are small, reddish and are borne in leafless spikes.

Flowering time May–August.

Distribution Widespread throughout lowland Europe.

Habitat Favours waste places and cultivated ground and often common on arable land.

### Fat-hen
*Chenopodium album*
SIZE AND DESCRIPTION  Up to 150 cm tall. A striking and upright annual. Dark green colour of plant is usually masked by covering of white, powdery meal. Stems sometimes have reddish streaks. Leaves vary in shape from narrow-oval to diamond-shaped and are 20–70 cm long; leaf margins are often toothed but are seldom lobed. Flowers are whitish and are borne in open, leafy spikes.
FLOWERING TIME  June–October.
DISTRIBUTION  Widespread throughout lowland Europe and often abundant in suitable locations.
HABITAT  Favours waste ground and disturbed arable land.

### Three-nerved sandwort
*Moehringia trinervia*
SIZE AND DESCRIPTION  Up to 5 cm tall. A rather delicate and downy annual with a straggling or trailing habit. Easily overlooked among larger woodland plants. Leaves are oval and pointed with three (sometimes five) distinct veins. Flowers are 5–6 mm across and comprise five white petals that are shorter than the five green sepals. Flowers are borne on slender stalks.
FLOWERING TIME  May–June.
DISTRIBUTION  Widespread throughout Europe but only locally common in suitable habitats.
HABITAT  Favours areas of rich, damp soils in relatively undisturbed woodland.

## Common chickweed
*Stellaria media*

SIZE AND DESCRIPTION  Up to 90 cm tall. A straggly and much-branched annual. Leaves are oval, fresh green in colour and borne in opposite pairs; upper leaves are unstalked. Flowers are 5–10 mm across and comprise five, white and deeply-divided petals that are shorter than the five green petals. Flowers borne on stalks.
FLOWERING TIME  Mainly July to November but can be found in flower in any month.
DISTRIBUTION  Widespread throughout Europe and often considered a persistent weed.
HABITAT  Favours disturbed ground and cultivated soils.

## Lesser stitchwort
*Stellaria graminea*

SIZE AND DESCRIPTION  Up to 50 cm tall. A straggly perennial, often found growing through grasses. Leaves are long, narrow and fresh green, closely resembling those of grasses. Flowers are 5–15 mm across and comprise five deeply cleft white petals and five green sepals of a similar length.
FLOWERING TIME  May–August.
DISTRIBUTION  Widespread throughout lowland Europe, except the far south.
HABITAT  Grassy places such as meadows and woodland rides. Favours acid soils, seldom occurs on lime.

## Sticky mouse-ear
*Cerastium glomeratum*
SIZE AND DESCRIPTION  Up to 40 cm tall. A
stickily-hairy annual. Leaves are oval, pointed
and are borne in opposite pairs. Stems are
often tinged red. Flowers are 10–15 mm
across and seldom open fully; they comprise
five white petals that are deeply notched and
five green sepals that are extremely hairy.
Flowers are borne in tight terminal clusters.
FLOWERING TIME  April–October.
DISTRIBUTION  Widespread throughout
lowland Europe, except for the north-east;
often abundant in suitable locations.
HABITAT  Favours dry, bare ground.

## White campion
*Silene lutifolia*
SIZE AND DESCRIPTION  Up to 1 m tall. An
upright and much-branched perennial
that is stickily-hairy all over. Leaves are
oval, usually stalkless and borne in opposite
pairs up the stem. Flowers are 25–30 mm
across and comprise five white petals that are
deeply notched. Flowers are borne in loose
clusters at the end of the stems.
FLOWERING TIME  May–October.
DISTRIBUTION  Widespread and locally common
throughout lowland Europe.
HABITAT  Favours hedgerows and grassy verges but also
occurs on recently disturbed and cultivated ground.

**Ragged robin**
*Lychnis flos-cuculi*
SIZE AND DESCRIPTION  Up to 80 cm
tall. An upright and distinctive perennial. Stems
are rough and sometimes branched. Stem leaves
are narrow, rough and grass-like; stalkless and
borne in opposite pairs. Basal leaves are stalked and
oblong. Flowers are pinkish-red and ragged-looking, comprising five
petals, each of which is divided into four lobes.
FLOWERING TIME  May–August.
DISTRIBUTION  Widespread and locally common throughout Europe;
least common in the south. Has declined due to land drainage.
HABITAT  Favours damp habitats such as fens, water meadows and
damp woodland rides.

## Red campion
*Silene dioica*

SIZE AND DESCRIPTION  Up to 1 m tall. An upright and downy biennial or perennial. Leaves are oval, hairy and borne in opposite pairs; those on the stems are usually stalkless. Flowers are 20–25 mm across and comprise five petals; these are usually deep pink but sometimes are much paler. Male and female flowers are borne on separate plants.

FLOWERING TIME  Mainly March to November but can be found in flower in any month.

DISTRIBUTION  Widespread throughout lowland Europe but least common in warmer southern areas.

HABITAT  Favours a wide variety of grassy habitats including woodland rides, meadows and roadside verges.

### Yellow water-lily
*Nymphaea lutea*
SIZE AND DESCRIPTION  A floating plant. A striking aquatic perennial with oval and leathery floating leaves that are heart-shaped at the base and up to 40 cm across; also has thinner, wavy-edged submerged leaves. Flowers are up to 6 cm across, with yellow overlapping sepals hiding the petals; borne on slender stalks above the water.
FLOWERING TIME  June–September.
DISTRIBUTION  Widespread throughout lowland Europe in suitable habitats.
HABITAT  Favours still or slow-flowing nutrient-rich water. Forms extensive carpets over the water surface in suitable locations.

## Marsh-marigold
*Caltha palustris*

SIZE AND DESCRIPTION  Up to 60 cm tall. A striking and distinctive hairless perennial with a creeping habit. Basal leaves are kidney-shaped, dark green and borne on long stalks. Stem leaves are smaller, more rounded and have shorter stalks. Flowers are 20–30 mm across and comprise five yellow sepals but no petals; borne in loose clusters.

FLOWERING TIME  March–July.

DISTRIUTION  Widespread throughout most of Europe but essentially absent from the Mediterranean region.

HABITAT  Favours damp ground and hence restricted to marshes, wet woodlands and fens.

## Wood anemone
*Anemone nemorosa*

SIZE AND DESCRIPTION  Up to 30 cm tall. A low-growing hairless perennial. Stem leaves are long-stalked and divided into three lobes, each of which is further divided. Flowers are up to 40 mm across and comprise five to ten whitish or pinkish petal-like sepals; flowers are solitary and borne on upright stalks.

FLOWERING TIME  March–May.

DISTRIBUTION  Widespread throughout much of Europe, absent from much of the Mediterranean.

HABITAT  Favours open woodlands across much of its range, often forming extensive carpets. Also alpine meadows.

## Meadow buttercup
*Ranunculus acris*

SIZE AND DESCRIPTION  Up to 1 m tall. A distinctive and familiar downy-hairy perennial. Leaves are divided into three to seven segments, each of which is oval or wedge-shaped, toothed and further divided. Flowers are 15–25 mm across and comprise five shiny yellow petals and five erect and green sepals. Flowers are borne on long stalks.

FLOWERING TIME  April–October.

DISTRIBUTION  Widespread throughout most of Europe.

HABITAT  Favours grassy habitats such as meadows and roadside verges. In favourable locations, often abundant.

## Pasqueflower
*Pulsatilla vulgaris*

SIZE AND DESCRIPTION  Up to 12 cm tall.
An attractive but low-growing hairy
perennial. Basal leaves are especially
hairy when they first appear; they are
much-divided into feathery segments
but these do not expand until the
flowers open. Bell-shaped
flowers are 55–85 mm
across and comprise six
purple segments surrounding
numerous yellow stamens.
Flowers are upright at first but become
nodding with maturity.
FLOWERING TIME  March–May.
DISTRIBUTION  Widespread but local
across central and north-west Europe.
Range much reduced by changes in
agricultural use.
HABITAT  Favours undisturbed ancient
grassland growing on lime-rich soils.

**Traveller's-joy**
*Clematis vitalba*
SIZE AND DESCRIPTION Up to 30 m
long. A vigorous and woody climber
with a rambling habit. Often smothers
shrubs through which it grows by the end of autumn. Leaves are pinnate
and divided into pointed leaflets. Flowers are 20 mm across and greenish-white;
borne in loose clusters. Fruits are reddish, feathery and distinctive.
FLOWERING TIME July–September.
DISTRIBUTION Widespread across much of central, southern and western Europe.
HABITAT Favours hedgerows, woodland margins and scrub habitats but almost
exclusively restricted to lime-rich soils.

## Common water-crowfoot
*Ranunculus aquatilis*

SIZE AND DESCRIPTION  Up to 1 m long. An attractive annual or perennial that, by the end of summer, often blankets the surface of the wetland habitats where it grows. Leaves are variable in appearance: surface leaves are rounded and toothed while submerged ones are finely-divided and thread-like. Flowers are 12–20 mm across and comprise five white petals.

FLOWERING TIME  April–August.

DISTRIBUTION  Widespread across most of lowland Europe.

HABITAT  Favours both slow-flowing streams and rivers and the still waters.

## Lesser celandine
*Ranunculus ficaria*

SIZE AND DESCRIPTION  Up to 30 cm tall. A low-growing perennial that, in favourable locations, often forms extensive carpets. Glossy dark green leaves are heart-shaped or kidney-shaped and borne on long stalks; sometimes appear rather variegated. Flowers are 15–30 mm across and borne on long stems; comprise three sepals and eight to twelve yellow petals. Flowers open fully only in bright sunshine.

FLOWERING TIME  March–May.

DISTRIBUTION  Widespread throughout most of Europe and sometimes locally abundant.

HABITAT  Favours open woodland and hedgerows.

## Common meadow-rue
*Thalictrum flavum*

SIZE AND DESCRIPTION Up to 1 m tall. A striking upright perennial. Fern-like leaves are divided into lobed leaflets. Flowers comprise four small whitish sepals and numerous protruding and erect yellow stamens, the latter resulting in a feathery appearance. Flowers are borne in dense clusters.

FLOWERING TIME June–July.

DISTRIBUTION Widespread throughout most of Europe, but usually distinctly local.

HABITAT Favours damp lowland habitats. Typically on base-rich soils. Also occurs locally in mountains.

## Common poppy
*Papaver rhoeas*

SIZE AND DESCRIPTION Up to 70 cm tall. A distinctive hairy annual. Leaves are divided into narrow toothed segments; only the lower leaves are stalked. Flowers are 60–90 mm across. They comprise two green sepals, that drop when flower opens, and bright red and papery petals. Fruit is a flat-topped capsule, the seeds released through pores beneath the cap.

FLOWERING TIME April–August.

DISTRIBUTION Widespread throughout Europe.

HABITAT Favours disturbed soil. In the absence of herbicides, often colours whole fields red.

## Yellow horned-poppy
*Glaucium flavum*
SIZE AND DESCRIPTION  Up to 90 cm
tall. A branching, clump-forming
biennial or perennial. Leaves are blue-
green, the basal ones being deeply
pinnately lobed and arranged in a rosette.
Flowers are 60–80 mm across and comprise
two sepals and four bright yellow papery petals.
The seed capsule is up to 30 cm long, slender and curved.
FLOWERING TIME  April–September.
DISTRIBUTION  Occurs on most suitable coasts around
Europe but generally only locally common.
HABITAT  Restricted to stable stretches of coastal sand and shingle.

### Garlic mustard
*Alliaria petiolata*
SIZE AND DESCRIPTION  Up to 1.2 m tall. An
upright patch-forming biennial. Leaves are
fresh green and heart-shaped with toothed
margins; they smell strongly of garlic when
crushed. Flowers are 4–6 mm across and
comprise four white petals; flowers borne in
clusters at stem tips. Fruits are slender pods,
which are ascending and up to 2 cm long.
FLOWERING TIME  April–July.
DISTRIBUTION  Widespread across most of
Europe in suitable habitats.
HABITAT  Favours hedgerows, woodland rides
and scrub habitats, invariably on lime-rich soils.

### Shepherd's-purse
*Capsella bursa-pastoris*
SIZE AND DESCRIPTION  Up to 40 cm tall. An
extremely variable upright annual or biennial. Has a
basal rosette of pinnately divided lobed leaves. Upper
leaves are toothed and clasp the stem. Flowers are
2–3 mm across and comprise four white petals and four
green hairy sepals. Flowers borne in terminal
heads at stem tips. Fruits are heart-shaped,
borne erect on stalks, and are 6–9 mm long.
FLOWERING TIME  Mainly April–October
but can be found in flower in any month.
DISTRIBUTION  Widespread throughout Europe.
HABITAT  Favours disturbed ground in gardens
and on tracks and arable land.

## Cuckoo flower or Lady's smock
*Cardamine pratensis*

SIZE AND DESCRIPTION  Up to 55 cm tall. An
attractive upright perennial. Has basal rosette
of pinnately divided leaves, comprising
one to seven pairs of rounded
leaflets. Flowers are 12–20 mm
across and comprise four whitish-
pink or pale lilac petals; borne in
open clusters at stem tips.
Fruits are narrow upright
pods up to 4 cm long.
FLOWERING TIME  April–July.
DISTRIBUTION  Widespread
throughout most of
Europe in suitable habitats.
HABITAT  Favours
permanently damp
ground in grassy
habitats such as
meadows, fens and
woodland rides.

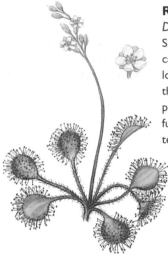

## Round-leaved sundew
*Drosera rotundifolia*
SIZE AND DESCRIPTION   Up to 8 cm tall. A distinctive carnivorous plant. Has a basal rosette of rounded, long-stalked leaves, covered with long, sticky hairs that trap insects and move to envelope and digest prey. Flowers are tiny, white and five-petalled; open fully only in bright sunshine. Flowers are borne terminally on upright, curved-tipped stalks.
FLOWERING TIME   June–August.
DISTRIBUTION   Widespread but local due to very specific habitat requirements; absent from Mediterranean islands and southern Iberia.
HABITAT   Waterlogged peaty soils in bogs, heaths.

## Charlock
*Sinapis arvensis*
SIZE AND DESCRIPTION   Up to 2 m tall. A striking and upright annual. Leaves are dark green or purplish-green and coarsely-toothed; lower ones are usually stalked while upper ones are stalkless and unlobed. Flowers are 15–20 mm across and comprise four yellow petals; sepals are green and down-turned. Flowers borne in dense terminal clusters. Fruits are long pods that have a beaded appearance.
FLOWERING TIME   April–October.
DISTRIBUTION   A native of southern Europe but introduced elsewhere and now widespread throughout most of the region.
HABITAT   Favours arable land and disturbed waste ground.

### Meadow saxifrage
*Saxifraga granulata*
SIZE AND DESCRIPTION  Up to 50 cm tall. An attractive
hairy perennial. Leaves are basal, kidney-shaped and
hairy with blunt teeth. Small brown bulbils are produced
at leaf bases in autumn and give rise to new plants. Flowers
are 20–30 mm across and comprise five white petals.
FLOWERING TIME  May–July.
DISTRIBUTION  Locally common in northern, central
and western Europe. In southern and eastern
Europe, confined to cool upland regions only.
HABITAT  Favours grassy meadows but also drier,
rocky sites, mostly on neutral to basic soils.

### Meadowsweet
*Filipendula ulmaria*
SIZE AND DESCRIPTION  Up to 2 m tall. A
striking upright perennial. Leaves are
pinnately divided into pairs of large,
toothed leaflets, interspersed with pairs
of much smaller ones. Flowers are
4–6 mm across and comprise five or six
creamy white petals; flowers borne in long,
frothy sprays up to 25 cm long.
FLOWERING TIME  June–September.
DISTRIBUTION  Widespread throughout most
of Europe although essentially absent from
the Mediterranean region.
HABITAT  Favours damp soils in meadows,
marshes and stream margins.

## Field-rose
*Rosa arvensis*

Size and description Up to 1 m
tall. A clump-forming shrub with trailing
or scrambling stems that carry curved thorns.
Leaves are divided into five to seven oval leaflets.
Flowers are 3–5 cm across and comprise five white petals;
flowers borne in open clusters of two to six blooms. Fruit is a
red ovoid hip.
Flowering time July–August.
Distribution Widespread in western and central Europe but scarce or
absent from the most northerly and southerly extremes of the region.
Habitat Favours woodland margins, hedgerows and scrub habitats.

## Dog-rose

*Rosa canina*

SIZE AND DESCRIPTION  Up to 5 m long. A scrambling deciduous shrub with erect or arched stems that are covered in hooked thorns. Leaves are pinnate and divided into five to seven leaflets. Flowers are 30–50 mm across and comprise five pink or whitish petals. Flowers often solitary but sometimes produced in small groups. Fruit is a bright red, 10–20 mm long, ovoid rosehip.

FLOWERING TIME  June–July.

DISTRIBUTION  Widespread throughout Europe except the far north.

HABITAT  Found in hedgerows, woodland margins and scrub habitats.

## Wood avens
*Geum urbanum*

SIZE AND DESCRIPTION  Up to 60 cm tall. A delicate and elegant hairy perennial. Basal leaves are pinnate and comprise one to five leaflets; stem leaves are three- to five-lobed. Flowers are 8–15 mm across and comprise five spreading yellow petals and five green sepals; flowers are erect at first but soon droop. Fruits are armed with hooked hairs for clinging to animal fur.

FLOWERING TIME  June–August.

DISTRIBUTION  Locally common throughout most of Europe in suitable habitats.

HABITAT  Favours shady woodland and hedgerows.

## Silverweed
*Potentilla anserina*

SIZE AND DESCRIPTION  Up to 80 cm long. A distinctive creeping perennial. Long-stalked leaves are silvery-green and comprise five to seven toothed and lobed leaflets. Leaves form a persistent basal rosette. Flowers are 5–20 mm across and typically comprise five bright yellow petals; flowers are borne on sprawling, radiating stems that root at the nodes.

FLOWERING TIME  June–September.

DISTRIBUTION  Widespread and common throughout most of Europe, except far south.

HABITAT  Favours a wide range of open habitats including bare grassy places, roadside verges, waste ground and coastal dunes.

## Tormentil
*Potentilla erecta*

SIZE AND DESCRIPTION  Up to 30 cm tall. A charming and delicate perennial. Upright and creeping stems typically found woven through other low-growing vegetation. Leaves are unstalked and trifoliate but appear five-lobed due to two leaflet-like stipules at the base. Flowers are 7–11 mm across and comprise four bright yellow petals. Petals are easily dislodged.

FLOWERING TIME  May–September.

DISTRIBUTION  Widespread throughout most of Europe.

HABITAT  Favours a wide range of grassy habitats including meadows, heaths and moors.

## Broom
*Cytisus scoparius*

SIZE AND DESCRIPTION  Up to 2 m tall. A much-branched, deciduous shrub with five-angled, ridged green stems. Stems typically erect but coastal forms are prostrate. Leaves are small and usually trifoliate. Flowers are 20 mm long and are borne on young shoots, either singly or in pairs. Fruits are flattened, oblong and hairy pods that ripen from green to black before exploding on sunny days to liberate seeds.

FLOWERING TIME  April–June.

DISTRIBUTION  Widespread throughout most of Europe.

HABITAT  Favours open woodland, heaths and coastal cliffs where dry, acid soils prevail.

## Common gorse
*Ulex europeaus*

SIZE AND DESCRIPTION Up to 2 m tall. A densely branched evergreen shrub. Twigs are greenish and almost leafless but bear numerous sharp spines, each of which is up to 25 mm long. Flowers are 15–25 mm long, bright yellow and coconut-scented. Fruits are hairy pods, which explode violently and audibly on sunny days liberating the seeds.

FLOWERING TIME April–May.

DISTRIBUTION Widespread native of western Europe; planted and naturalised elsewhere.

HABITAT Favours heaths, rough grassland and coastal cliffs on acid soils.

## Tufted vetch
*Vicia cracca*

SIZE AND DESCRIPTION Up to 2 m tall. An elegant, scrambling perennial that climbs by means of tendrils and often smothers the vegetation that it grows through by. late summer. Leaves are pinnately divided into six to 15 leaflets and end in branched tendrils. Flowers are bluish-purple and borne in stalked spikes up to 10 cm long. Fruits are brown, hairless pods.

FLOWERING TIME June–August.

DISTRIBUTION Widespread and locally throughout most of Europe.

HABITAT Favours grassy and scrub habitats including meadows and hedgerows.

## Common vetch
*Vicia sativa*

SIZE AND DESCRIPTION
Up to 75 cm tall. A rather
delicate-looking, downy
annual that scrambles through
other low-growing vegetation.
Leaves comprise three to eight
pairs of oval leaflets and end in
tendrils. Flowers are 20–30 mm long and pinkish-
purple; borne in groups of one or two. Pods are blackish when ripe.
FLOWERING TIME April–September.
DISTRIBUTION Exact status difficult to determine. Widespread as a native
species throughout most of lowland Europe except the far north. Also
cultivated for fodder and naturalised in many parts.
HABITAT Favours all sorts of grassy habitats.

## Common restharrow
*Ononis repens*

SIZE AND DESCRIPTION  Up to 70 cm tall. A robust perennial under-shrub with hairy stems that may be either spreading or upright. The whole plant has a foetid smell when rubbed. Stems sometimes bear soft spines. Leaves are stickily-hairy and usually trifoliate with oval leaflets. Flowers are 10–15 mm long, pink and white, and borne in clusters. Fruits are small pods up to 7 mm long.

FLOWERING TIME  July–September.

DISTRIBUTION  Locally common in western, south-western and central Europe.

HABITAT  Restricted to dry grassy places on calcareous soils.

## Black medick
*Medicago lupulina*

SIZE AND DESCRIPTION  Up to 20 cm tall. A low-growing and often trailing downy annual; sometimes a short-lived perennial. Leaves are trifoliate, with each leaflet having a point at the centre of its apex. Flowers are 2–3 mm long and borne in densely packed rounded clusters that are carried on long stalks. Pods are kidney-shaped and black when ripe.

FLOWERING TIME  April–October.

DISTRIBUTION  Widespread throughout most of lowland Europe. Sometimes cultivated for fodder.

HABITAT  Favours dry grassy places and disturbed ground.

## White clover
*Trifolium repens*
SIZE AND DESCRIPTION  Up to 20 cm tall. A hairless perennial with prostrate, branching stems that root and form extensive mats. Leaves are trifoliate and borne on upright stems; leaflets are ovate with a white mark and darker veins. Flowers are borne in rounded heads, 2 cm across; flowers are usually whitish but sometimes are tinged pink.
FLOWERING TIME  April–October.
DISTRIBUTION  Widespread across most of Europe. Locally abundant.
HABITAT  Favours a wide range of grassy habitats.

## Common bird's-foot-trefoil
*Lotus corniculatus*
SIZE AND DESCRIPTION  Up to 35 cm tall. A variable perennial that may be hairy or hairless and can have a creeping or ascending habit. Leaves are grey-green and downy; they comprise five leaflets, although they appear trifoliate. Flowers are 10–16 mm long and usually yellow, tinged reddish; borne on stalked heads of two to seven flowers. Fruits are slender pods, 15–30 mm long, which are splayed like the toes of a bird's foot.
FLOWERING TIME  April–September.
DISTRIBUTION  Widespread and often common throughout most of Europe in suitable habitats.
HABITAT  Favours all sorts of grassy habitats and tolerates a wide range of soil types.

## Kidney vetch
*Anthyllis vulneraria*

SIZE AND DESCRIPTION

Up to 90 cm tall. A variable
silky hairy annual, biennial or
perennial. Leaves are pinnately divided into
one to seven pairs of narrow leaflets. Flowers
are usually deep yellow although purple, red
and orange forms are not uncommon; borne
in long-stalked kidney-shaped clustered heads,
3 cm across. Ripe pods are brown.

FLOWERING TIME April–September.

DISTRIBUTION Widespread across almost the
whole of Europe.

HABITAT Favours all sorts of grassy and rocky
habitats on calcareous soils, from coastal cliffs
to chalk downland and mountain pastures.

## Wood-sorrel
*Oxalis acetosella*
SIZE AND DESCRIPTION  Up to 10 cm tall. A downy
perennial with a creeping habit. Leaves are trefoil
and shamrock-like; borne on long stalks in the
form of a rosette. Leaves fold down at night.
Flowers are solitary, 8–15 mm across and
borne on slender stalks; petals usually white
with purple veins but sometimes tinged purple.
FLOWERING TIME  April–May.
DISTRIBUTION  Widespread and locally common
in most parts of Europe.
HABITAT  Favours undisturbed woodland and
hedgerows. Common under oak and beech.

## Herb-Robert
*Geranium robertianum*
SIZE AND DESCRIPTION  Up to 30 cm tall.
A straggling and rather delicate
annual. The whole plant is strong
smelling and is sometimes tinged red.
Leaves are hairy and deeply cut into
three or five lobes. Flowers are 12–15 mm
across, five-petalled and pink; flowers borne in
loose clusters on long stalks. The fruits are hairy.
FLOWERING TIME  April–October.
DISTRIBUTION  Widespread throughout the
whole of Europe, absent far north.
HABITAT  Favours shady places such as rocky
banks, hedgerows and woodlands.

### Meadow crane's-bill
*Geranium pratense*

SIZE AND DESCRIPTION Up to 80 cm tall. A striking, branched and hairy perennial. Leaves are divided into five to seven ovate and deeply cut lobes. Flowers are 30–40 mm across and comprise five rounded and bluish-violet petals with darker veins; flowers are borne in compact clusters, which droop after flowering.

FLOWERING TIME June–September.

DISTRIBUTION Widespread and locally common across much of Europe but rare in Mediterranean and northern regions.

HABITAT Favours meadows and roadside verges, usually on base-rich soils.

## Fairy flax
*Linum catharticum*
SIZE AND DESCRIPTION Up to 15 cm tall.
A rather delicate annual. Leaves are
lanceolate, single veined and borne in
opposite pairs. Flowers are up to 6 mm
across and comprise five white petals;
flowers are borne on long, slender
stalks that are nodding in bud.
FLOWERING TIME May–September.
DISTRIBUTION Widespread across most
of Europe but local; occurs only in
upland areas in the south.
HABITAT Favours a range of grassy
habitats, both wet and dry, but almost
always on calcareous soils.

## Dog's mercury
*Mercurialis perennis*
SIZE AND DESCRIPTION Up to 50 cm tall. An upright
and unbranched downy-hairy perennial. Leaves
are shiny, dark green and ovate-lanceolate
with toothed margins; most leaves are borne
on upper part of plant. Clusters of rather
insignificant greenish flowers are borne on upright
spikes. Male and female flowers on separate plants.
FLOWERING TIME March–May.
DISTRIBUTION Widespread across most
of Europe except the far north.
HABITAT Woodlands, especially under
oak or beech, sometimes abundant.

## Sun spurge
*Euphorbia helioscopia*
SIZE AND DESCRIPTION  Up to 50 cm tall.
An upright hairless annual. Upright
stems bear fleshy spoon-shaped leaves,
broadest near the tip. Flowers are yellow;
they lack both petals and sepals, instead
comprise oval green glands. Umbel has
five green bracts. Fruits are smooth.
FLOWERING TIME  April–November.
DISTRIBUTION  Widespread throughout
the whole of Europe, often abundant in
suitable locations.
HABITAT  Found on arable land, waste
ground and cultivated soils.

## Common milkwort
*Polygala vulgaris*
SIZE AND DESCRIPTION  Up to 30 cm
tall. A delicate perennial, which has
either a trailing or an upright habit.
Leaves are alternate; lower ones are
oval while upper ones are narrow and
pointed. Flowers are 6–8 mm long and can
be blue, pink or white; borne in clustered
terminal spikes of 10 to 40 flowers.
FLOWERING TIME  June–September.
DISTRIBUTION  Widespread across most
of Europe.
HABITAT  Favours a variety of grassy habitats
and found on all but the most acidic of soils.

## Hairy St John's-wort
*Hypericum hirsutum*
SIZE AND DESCRIPTION Height up to 1 m.
An upright downy perennial with round
stems. Leaves are hairy, oblong to
elliptical, and are borne in opposite pairs.
Flowers are 15 mm across and comprise five
yellow petals; the five sepals are shorter than the
petals and are pointed with black glands on margins.
FLOWERING TIME June–September.
DISTRIBUTION Widespread across most of Europe
although absent from much of the south and
north-east.
HABITAT Favours damp grassy areas, especially
along woodland rides.

## Common mallow
*Malva sylvestris*

SIZE AND DESCRIPTION  Up to 1.5 m tall. A rather variable perennial that may be either upright or spreading in habit. Leaves are rounded at the base but five-lobed on the stem. Flowers are 25–40 mm across and comprise five pink petals that have purple veins and are hairy at the base.

FLOWERING TIME  June–September.

DISTRIBUTION  Widespread and common throughout Europe.

HABITAT  Favours grassy places such as meadows and roadside verges, often thriving best in disturbed soil.

## Common dog-violet
*Viola riviniana*

SIZE AND DESCRIPTION  Up to 15 cm tall. An almost hairless perennial. Leaves are long-stalked, heart-shaped, blunt-tipped and up to 4 cm long. Flowers are 10–13 mm across. The blue-violet petals are broad and unequal, and are marked with dark veins towards the flower centre; the lower petal has a pale lilac spur, 3–5 mm long.

FLOWERING TIME  March–May.

DISTRIBUTION  Widespread across most of Europe, except the south-east.

HABITAT  Favours woodland rides and grassy places.

## Heartsease or Wild pansy
*Viola tricolor*

SIZE AND DESCRIPTION Up to 40 cm tall. A branching hairless or downy-hairy annual, biennial or perennial. Lower leaves are ovate while upper ones are oblong; the stipules are deeply divided. Flowers are 10–15 mm across; petals are unequal and yellow, violet or bicoloured; lower one bears a spur, 6 mm long. Sepals are longer than petals.

FLOWERING TIME April–November.

DISTRIBUTION Most of Europe.

HABITAT Favours cultivated ground and grassland.

## Purple-loosestrife
*Lythrum salicaria*

SIZE AND DESCRIPTION Up to 1.5 m tall. A downy perennial. Upright stems carry narrow and unstalked leaves either as opposite pairs or in whorls of three. Flowers are 10–15 mm across and borne in tight whorls creating a tall spike; the petals are reddish-purple and there are 12 stamens.

FLOWERING TIME June–August.

DISTRIBUTION Widespread across Europe. Absent far north.

HABITAT Favours damp ground, typically grows beside water. Forms extensive stands in suitable locations.

### Enchanter's-nightshade
*Circaea lutetiana*
SIZE AND DESCRIPTION  Up to 60 cm tall. A delicate, creeping perennial. Upright stems are sometimes slightly hairy and carry opposite pairs of ovate, pointed leaves that are heart-shaped or rounded at the base, up to 10 cm long. Flowers are 4–8 mm and comprise two white and deeply-divided petals; flowers are borne in a loose spike above leaves.
FLOWERING TIME  June-September.
DISTRIBUTION  Widespread across most of Europe except the north-east.
HABITAT  Likes woodlands, hedgerows.

### Rosebay willowherb
*Chamerion angustifolium*
SIZE AND DESCRIPTION  1.5 m tall. A showy, upright perennial. Leaves are lanceolate and arranged spirally up the stem. Flowers are 20–30 mm across and comprise four pinkish petals, which are slightly unequal. Seeds are small but possess a long plume of silky white hairs, which assists in wind dispersal.
FLOWERING TIME  June–August.
DISTRIBUTION  Widespread throughout most of Europe except the north.
HABITAT  Favours a wide range of disturbed ground. Forms large clumps.

## Great willowherb
*Epilobium hirsutum*
SIZE AND DESCRIPTION
Up to 2 m tall. An
impressive downy or
hairy perennial. Leaves
are stalkless and
opposite and lanceolate
to oblong; they are toothed
and clasp the stem at the base. The
flowers are 15–25 mm across and
comprise four pinkish-purple petals
that are equal, notched at the tip and have pale centres.
FLOWERING TIME June–August.
DISTRIBUTION Widespread across most of Europe. Absent far north.
HABITAT Favours damp soils in fens, marshes and the margins of
rivers. Often forms extensive and sizeable clumps.

## Sea-holly

*Eryngium maritimum*

SIZE AND DESCRIPTION  Up to 60
cm tall. An intriguing and
distinctive perennial. Leaves are
bluish-green, leathery and ovate with
sharp spines that give them a holly-like
appearance; basal leaves are stalked
while stem leaves are stalkless.
Flowers are small and blue; borne
in globular umbels up to 2 cm
across, with spiny bracts below.
FLOWERING TIME  June–September.
DISTRIBUTION  Widespread on
suitable habitats all around the
coast of Europe
except the north.
HABITAT  Restricted to stable
and undisturbed coastal sand
and shingle.

## Cow parsley
*Anthriscus sylvestris*
SIZE AND DESCRIPTION Up to 1 m tall. An upright and downy, perennial herb. Upright, hollow and ridged stem is purple and carries leaves that are two or three times pinnately divided. Flowers are small and white and borne in flattened umbels that lack lower bracts. Fruits are black.
FLOWERING TIME April–June.
DISTRIBUTION Most of Europe.
HABITAT Favours grassy places such as roadside verges, woodland margins and lanes. Forms extensive patches in suitable locations.

## Hemlock
*Conium maculatum*
SIZE AND DESCRIPTION Up to 2 m tall. An impressive and distinctive upright perennial, all parts of which are highly poisonous. Stem is hollow, ridged and blotched purple. Leaves are up to four times pinnately divided into fine leaflets. Flowers are small and white; borne in umbels up to 5 cm across.
FLOWERING TIME June–August.
DISTRIBUTION Widespread across most of Europe, except the far north.
HABITAT Favours damp wayside ground and often found along river margins or on waste ground.

## Hogweed
*Heracleum sphondylium*
SIZE AND DESCRIPTION Up to 4 m tall. An extremely robust and impressive perennial. Stem is stout, hollow and hairy. Leaves are up to 60 cm long; they are broad, hairy and usually pinnately divided into up to nine toothed segments. Flowers are small, off-white and with unequal petals; borne in slightly domed umbels up to 20 cm across.
FLOWERING TIME April–November.
DISTRIBUTION Widespread across much of Europe except the Mediterranean and the far north.
HABITAT Favours open grassy places such as meadows and roadside verges.

## Heather
*Calluna vulgaris*

Size and description  Up to 1.5 m tall. A much-branched, dense undershrub, often referred to as "ling". Leaves are short, narrow and scale-like; borne in four rows along stems. Flowers are 4–5 mm long, pinkish but sometimes almost white; borne in long terminal spikes.

Flowering time  July–September.

Distribution  Widespread across much of Europe in suitable habitats. Absent from most of the Mediterranean.

Habitat  Restricted to acid soils on heath and moors. In suitable locations, can form extensive ground cover.

## Bilberry
*Vaccinium myrtillus*

Size and description  Up to 60 cm tall. An upright, much-branched deciduous shrub. Leaves are oval and bright green; borne on twigs that are green and three-angled. Flowers are 4–6 mm across and greenish-pink; eventually ripen to form a blue-black berry 6–10 mm across. Also called whortleberries, fruits are delicious to eat.

Flowering time  April–June.

Distribution  Widespread across much of Europe but restricted to upland regions in the south.

Habitat  Confined to heaths, moors and woodlands on acid soils.

## Bell heather
*Erica cinerea*

SIZE AND DESCRIPTION
Up to 50 cm tall. A
hairless and evergreen
undershrub. Leaves are
narrow and needle-like; borne in
whorls of three up the wiry stems.
Flowers are 5–6 mm long, bell-shaped
and purplish-red; appear in open clusters
towards the stem tips.

FLOWERING TIME June–September.

DISTRIBUTION Widespread in western Europe in suitable
habitats but also occurs more locally as far north as southern
Scandinavia and as far south as northern Italy.

HABITAT Restricted to dry acid soils on heaths and moors.

## Scarlet pimpernel
*Anagallis arvensis*

SIZE AND DESCRIPTION  Up to 50 cm long. A prostrate and almost hairless annual. Leaves are ovate to lanceolate and 8–10 mm long; borne as opposite pairs along branching stems. Flowers are 12–15 mm across, comprise five lobes and are carried singly on long slender stalks; usually scarlet but sometimes pink or blue. Flowers close by early afternoon or in dull weather.

FLOWERING TIME  March–October.

DISTRIBUTION  Widespread throughout almost all of Europe.

HABITAT  Favours disturbed and cultivated ground. Can become locally abundant.

## Primrose
*Primula vulgaris*

SIZE AND DESCRIPTION  Up to 20 cm tall. A charming and familiar, clump forming, hairy perennial. Leaves are oval and tapering, up to 12 cm long, and form a rosette. Flowers are 2–3 cm across and comprise five lobes that are usually pale yellow; flowers are solitary and borne on long, hairy stalks arising from the centre of the leaf rosette.

FLOWERING TIME  March–June.

DISTRIBUTION  Widespread and locally common across much of Europe.

HABITAT  Favours woodland rides and margins, shady meadows and hedgerows.

## Cowslip
*Primula veris*

SIZE AND
DESCRIPTION  Up to
25 cm tall. A charming
perennial. Leaves are
hairy and tapering, similar
to those of primrose but
more wrinkled; they form a basal
rosette. Flowers are orange-yellow,
bell-shaped and 8–15 mm across;
borne in drooping, one-sided heads on
long, upright and naked stalks.
FLOWERING TIME  April–June.
DISTRIBUTION  Widespread and locally
across much of Europe except the far
north and south of the region.
HABITAT  Favours grassland, open woodland
rides and scrub but restricted to areas of
lime- and chalk-rich soils.

## Common centaury
*Centaurium erythraea*
SIZE AND DESCRIPTION Up to 50 cm tall. An attractive and slender, upright perennial. Leaves are ovate; they form a basal rosette and also appear as opposite pairs up the stems. Flowers are 5–15 mm across and comprise five pink petal lobes. Flowers are borne in loose clusters near the stem tops and open fully only in bright sunshine.
FLOWERING TIME April–September.
DISTRIBUTION Widespread across almost the whole of Europe.
HABITAT Favours dry, grassy places, stony ground and sand dunes.

## Thrift
*Armeria maritima*
SIZE AND DESCRIPTION Up to 60 cm tall. A distinctive cushion-forming perennial. Leaves are narrow, grass-like and up to 15 cm long; they arise as numerous rosettes from woody base of the plant. Flowers are pink and borne in heads 1–3 cm across on slender and erect leafless stalks.
FLOWERING TIME Mainly May–June, occasionally from April–October.
DISTRIBUTION Widespread and often locally abundant around coasts throughout Europe.
HABITAT Favours coastal cliffs and saltmarshes but also occasionally found on mountaintops.

## Lady's bedstraw
*Galium verum*

SIZE AND DESCRIPTION Up to 1.2 m long. A trailing and sprawling branched perennial. Leaves are narrow and have rolled margins; borne in whorls of eight to twelve along four-angled stems. Leaves blacken when dry. Flowers are 2–3 mm across and comprise four bright yellow petal lobes; produced in dense clusters at the ends of much-branched stems.

FLOWERING TIME June–September.

DISTRIBUTION Widespread throughout much of Europe, except the far north.

HABITAT Favours dry, grassy habitats.

## Field bindweed
*Convolvulus arvensis*

SIZE AND DESCRIPTION Up to 2 m long. A creeping and climbing perennial that uses its stems to twist around other plants. Leaves are 2–5 cm long and arrow-shaped with backward-pointing basal lobes. Flowers are 3 cm across, trumpet-shaped and may be white, pink or longitudinally striped; borne in stalked clusters arising from leaf axils.

FLOWERING TIME June–September.

DISTRIBUTION Widespread and common across most of Europe.

HABITAT Favours cultivated ground, roadside verges, disturbed land. Often considered an agricultural weed.

## Viper's-bugloss
*Echium vulgare*

SIZE AND DESCRIPTION Up to 90 cm tall.
A striking and roughly hairy biennial,
which is slightly hispid. Leaves are
narrow and pointed, up to 15 cm long
and the basal ones are stalked. Flowers
are 15–20 mm long, funnel-shaped and
bright blue; they are borne in tall
upright spikes or shorter
downcurved sprays.

FLOWERING TIME May–September.

DISTRIBUTION Widespread and locally
common throughout most of Europe.

HABITAT Favours dry, grassy habitats,
especially on chalky or sandy ground
and often near the coast.

## Common comfrey
*Symphytum officinale*

SIZE AND DESCRIPTION Up to 1.2 m tall. An upright and hairy perennial. Basal leaves are oval, hairy and up to 25 cm long; stem leaves are shorter and often clasp the stems. Flowers are 13–19 mm long, tubular and bell-shaped; colour variable but usually creamy white or pinkish-purple. Flowers are borne in curved clusters.

FLOWERING TIME May–June.

DISTRIBUTION Widespread across most of Europe in suitable habitats.

HABITAT Favours damp ground and often found growing beside rivers or in fens and marshes.

## Water forget-me-not
*Myosotis scorpioides*

SIZE AND DESCRIPTION Up to 12 cm tall. A creeping and usually hairless perennial. Leaves are oblong to lanceolate in outline and are borne on upright stems. Flowers are up to 8 mm across and comprise five joined petals that are blue with a central yellow eye; borne in terminal clusters.

FLOWERING TIME May–September.

DISTRIBUTION Widespread across northern, western and central Europe.

HABITAT Restricted to watery habitats on neutral and basic soils beside rivers and in marshes.

## Wood sage
*Teucrium scorodonia*

SIZE AND DESCRIPTION  Up to 50 cm tall. A striking, hairy perennial with upright branched stems. Sometimes forms sizeable clumps. Leaves are stalked, ovate to heart-shaped, wrinkled and sage-like. Flowers are up to 9 mm long and greenish-yellow; paired and borne on upright spikes up to 15 cm long.

FLOWERING TIME  July–September.

DISTRIBUTION  Widespread and locally common in western, southern and central parts. As far north as the Baltic.

HABITAT  Favours woodland rides, heaths and coastal cliffs on acid soils.

## White dead-nettle
*Lamium album*

SIZE AND DESCRIPTION  Up to 80 cm tall. A hairy and slightly aromatic perennial. In the absence of flowers, resembles common nettle, but unrelated to that species and stingless. Leaves are ovate to heart-shaped, nettle-like and appear as opposite pairs on the stems. Flowers are 20–25 mm long and white with a hooded upper lip; borne in dense whorls.

FLOWERING TIME  March–December.

DISTRIBUTION  Widespread in much of Europe although scarce in the south.

HABITAT  Favours roadside verges, hedgerows and woodland margins.

### Yellow archangel
*Lamiastrum galeobdolon*

SIZE AND DESCRIPTION Up to 45 cm tall.
A creeping and patch-forming hairy
perennial with upright flowering stems.
Leaves are nettle-like, toothed and
oval, and borne in opposite pairs.
Flowers are 15–25 mm long and bright
yellow with a hooded upper lip; borne
in whorls around the stem.

FLOWERING TIME May–June.

DISTRIBUTION Widespread and locally
common in much of Europe in
suitable habitats.

HABITAT Favours woodlands,
hedgerows and other shady places.
Usually found on basic soils. Can form
sizeable clumps in suitable locations.

## Selfheal
*Prunella vulgaris*
SIZE AND DESCRIPTION  Up to 20 cm tall. A creeping and mat-forming downy perennial that is popular with insects. Leaves are oval, 5 cm long and sometimes bluntly toothed; borne in opposite pairs. Flowers are 13–15 mm long, two-lipped and violet-blue; borne in short, dense and cylindrical heads. Flower bracts persist after flowers have dropped.
FLOWERING TIME  March–November.
DISTRIBUTION  Widespread and often common across much of Europe.
HABITAT  Meadows, grassy woodland rides, on calcareous or neutral soils.

## Wild thyme
*Thymus polytrichus*
SIZE AND DESCRIPTION  Up to 5 cm tall. An aromatic, creeping perennial that often forms extensive carpets. Leaves are ovate to circular and short-stalked; borne in opposite pairs along the wiry stems. Flowers are 7–12 mm long, two-lipped and pinkish-purple. Borne in dense terminal heads.
FLOWERING TIME  April–August.
DISTRIBUTION  Widespread and locally common across most of central, western and southern Europe.
HABITAT  Favours free-draining sites such as dry grassland and heaths; also found on coastal sand dunes and cliffs.

## Great mullein
*Verbascum thapsus*
SIZE AND DESCRIPTION Up to 2 m tall. A robust biennial, covered in white woolly hairs. Basal leaves are elliptical and up to 50 cm long; they form a rosette in the first year. Stem leaves have stalks running down to winged stems. Flowers are 12–35 mm across and comprise five yellow lobes; borne in dense, usually unbranched spikes.
FLOWERING TIME June–August.
DISTRIBUTION Widespread across most of Europe, far north and south-east.
HABITAT Favours dry, grassy places, roadside verges and waste ground.

## Wild clary
*Salvia verbenaca*
SIZE AND DESCRIPTION Up to 80 cm tall. An upright and downy perennial. Basal leaves are oval, sometimes pinnately lobed and with jagged-toothed margins; they form a rosette. Stem leaves are smaller and, together with the bracts, they are purplish. Flowers are 6–10 mm long and variable in colour, but usually blue or violet.
FLOWERING TIME April–September.
DISTRIBUTION Widespread and local in western and southern Europe.
HABITAT Dry grassy habitats, often coastal, invariably on lime-rich soils.

## Common figwort
*Scrophularia nodosa*

SIZE AND DESCRIPTION Up to 70 cm tall. A hairless perennial, which is foetid-smelling when rubbed. Stems square in cross-section and typically are not winged. Leaves are short-stalked, oval and pointed with sharp-toothed margins. Flowers are 7–10 mm across, two-lipped and green with maroon-brown lips; borne in open, branched spikes. Fruits are green.

FLOWERING TIME June–September.

DISTRIBUTION Widespread across central, western and southern Europe.

HABITAT Favours damp woodland and shady verges and hedgerows.

## Common toadflax
*Linaria vulgaris*

SIZE AND DESCRIPTION Up to 90 cm tall. An essentially hairless, grey-green perennial with upright stems arising from a creeping stock. Leaves are linear or lanceolate, alternate and crowded. Flowers are 25–35 mm across, two-lipped and usually bright yellow; the lower lip has an orange spot and a straight and long spur.

FLOWERING TIME June–October.

DISTRIBUTION Widespread across much of Europe except the Mediterranean region and the far north.

HABITAT Favours dry grassy places, waste ground, hedgerows and verges.

### Foxglove
*Digitalis purpurea*

SIZE AND DESCRIPTION Up to 1.8 m tall. A tall and elegant greyish biennial, or short-lived perennial. Leaves are ovate to lanceolate, long-stalked and softly hairy; in the first year they form a basal rosette from which the flower spike arises in the second year. Flowers are 40–55 mm long, tubular and borne on dense spikes. Extremely popular with pollinating insects.

FLOWERING TIME June–September.

DISTRIBUTION Widespread across much of western Europe.

HABITAT Favours woodlands, moors and sea cliffs, usually on acid soils.

## Heath speedwell
*Veronica officinalis*

SIZE AND DESCRIPTION  Up to 10 cm tall.
Low-growing perennial with a mat-forming habit.
Prostrate stems root at the nodes and are hairy all
round. Leaves are stalked, ovate to elliptical,
toothed and softly hairy. Flowers are 8 mm across,
lilac-blue with dark veins, and comprise four equal
sepal lobes and four unequal petal lobes.
FLOWERING TIME  May–August.
DISTRIBUTION  Widespread and locally common
across most of Europe.
HABITAT  Grassy woodland rides and
dry heathland areas.

## Brooklime
*Veronica beccabunga*

SIZE AND DESCRIPTION  Up to 30 cm tall. A hairless
perennial with creeping and rooting stems, which
become upright. Leaves are oval and fleshy, and
borne on short stalks. Flowers are 7–8 mm
across and blue with a white centre; borne in
pairs arising from leaf axils.
FLOWERING TIME  May–September.
DISTRIBUTION  Widespread in suitable habitats
across Europe except far north and drier
Mediterranean regions.
HABITAT  Restricted to shallow water
and damp soil beside rivers and ponds.

## Common cow-wheat
*Melampyrum pratense*

SIZE AND DESCRIPTION  Up to 50 cm tall. A variable hairless or slightly downy annual that sometimes is branched, and which has an upright habit. A semi-parasite of grassland plants. Leaves are narrow and shiny and are borne in opposite pairs. Flowers are 10–18 mm long, two-lipped and tubular and bright yellow; flowers arise from leaf axils.

FLOWERING TIME May–September.

DISTRIBUTION  Widespread across most of Europe.

HABITAT  Favours grassy woodland rides and grassy heaths; found mainly on acid soils.

## Marsh lousewort
*Pedicularis palustris*
SIZE AND DESCRIPTION  Up to 20 cm tall. A
spreading perennial that is branched from the
base. A semi-parasite of wetland plants. Leaves
are alternate and feathery but vary in outline
from roughly triangular or lanceolate to pinnately
lobed and toothed. Flowers are 13–15 mm long,
pink and two-lipped with a straight corolla.
FLOWERING TIME  April–July.
DISTRIBUTION  Widespread but local in western
and central Europe.
HABITAT  Damp heaths and moors on
nutrient-poor acid soils.

## Yellow-rattle
*Rhinanthus minor*
SIZE AND DESCRIPTION  Up to 50 cm tall. A
branched and hairy or hairless annual that
is a characteristic component of many
meadows. A semi-parasite of grassland plants.
Stems are black-spotted. Leaves are opposite and
oblong with rounded teeth. Flowers are 1–2 cm
long, yellow and borne in leafy terminal spikes.
Seeds rattle inside ripe fruit.
FLOWERING TIME  May–September.
DISTRIBUTION  Common across much of Europe
except Mediterranean region.
HABITAT  Rough grassy places.

## Black nightshade
*Solanum nigrum*
SIZE AND DESCRIPTION Up to 70 cm
tall. A straggling or upright
branching annual that may be
hairless or downy. Leaves are oval
and pointed, short-stalked, and up to
3–6 mm long. Flowers are 7–12 mm across
with five white lobes and yellow anthers that form
a projecting cone. Berries are rounded and 6–10 mm across,
green at first but ripening black. Berries are poisonous.
FLOWERING TIME January–October.
DISTRIBUTION Widespread across most of Europe and often common.
HABITAT Favours disturbed ground and cultivated land, including gardens.

## Common broomrape
*Orobanche minor*

SIZE AND DESCRIPTION  Up to 40 cm tall.
A distinctive upright annual that is
parasitic on the roots of clovers and
other herbaceous plants. Plant totally
lacks chlorophyll. Leaves are reduced
to brownish scales on the stem.
Flowers are 10–18 mm long, two-
lipped and tubular; colour variable
but usually pinkish-yellow and
purple-veined.

FLOWERING TIME  June–September.

DISTRIBUTION  Widespread across
most of central, western and
southern Europe.

HABITAT  Favours a wide range of
grassy habitats where suitable host
plants flourish.

*Dipsacaceae*

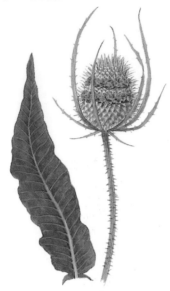

## Wild teasel
*Dipsacus fullonum*

SIZE AND DESCRIPTION  Up to 2 m tall. A hairless biennial whose stout stems are armed with sharp prickles. Produces rosettes of elliptical or oblong, spine-covered leaves in the first year. In the second year, tall branching stems are produced with narrower stem leaves. Flowers are purple and borne in spiny conical heads; the heads persist in seed.

FLOWERING TIME  July–August.

DISTRIBUTION  Widespread in western, southern and central Europe.

HABITAT  Favours grassland on damp, disturbed soils.

## Field scabious
*Knautia arvensis*

SIZE AND DESCRIPTION  Up to 1 m tall. A hairy biennial. Basal leaves are pinnately lobed or entire and form a basal rosette. Stem leaves are pinnately divided into up to 16 narrow lobes and a broader terminal one. Flowers are small and pink or lilac; borne in flat-topped heads 15–40 mm across; petals of outer flowers larger than those of inner ones.

FLOWERING TIME  June–October.

DISTRIBUTION  Most of Europe, absent from the Mediterranean region.

HABITAT  Favours grassy places; usually only on calcareous soils.

## Creeping bellflower
*Campanula rapunculoides*
SIZE AND DESCRIPTION  Up to 1 m tall. An
upright and clump-forming perennial
that may be downy or hairless. Spreads
by means of creeping rootstock. Basal
leaves are ovate, heart-shaped at the
base and long-stalked. Stem leaves are narrower
and unstalked. Flowers are 2–3 cm long, bell-
shaped and bluish-violet; borne in tall spikes.
FLOWERING TIME  June–September.
DISTRIBUTION  Widespread and locally in central
and western Europe; naturalised as a garden
escape in Britain.
HABITAT  Favours grassy places including
roadside verges and meadows.

## Hemp-agrimony
*Eupatorium cannabinum*

Size and description  Up to 1.75 m
tall. A distinctive and upright, downy
perennial. Stems are often
reddish. Leaves are divided
into three or five lobes and
are borne in opposite
pairs up the stems.
Flowers are dull pink and
small; grouped in dense clusters 2–5 mm across,
which are borne in loose terminal inflorescences.
Seeds are wind-dispersed, aided by feathery white hairs.
Flowering time  July–September.
Distribution  Widespread in suitable habitats across most of
Europe except the far north.
Habitat  Typically favours damp ground such as fens and
marshes; occasionally in drier situations.

## Common ragwort

*Senecio jacobaea*

SIZE AND DESCRIPTION  Up to 1 m tall. An invasive and usually hairless biennial or perennial, the whole of which is highly poisonous. Plant often covered in orange and black striped caterpillars of cinnabar moth. Leaves are pinnately divided with a blunt end lobe. Flower heads area 15–25 mm across and are bright yellow; borne in flat-topped clusters.

FLOWERING TIME  June–November.

DISTRIBUTION  Widespread across most of Europe although essentially absent from the north.

HABITAT  Favours dry grassy places and verges. Avoided by grazing animals and hence often thrives in pastures. Leaves contains an alkaloid poison, which can damage livestock over a period of time.

## Scentless mayweed
*Tripleurospermum inodorum*

SIZE AND DESCRIPTION  Up to 75 cm. A scentless and hairless annual or perennial that is much-branched. Leaves are alternate, much divided and feathery. Flower heads are 2–4 cm across and daisy-like, comprising densely-packed small yellow disc florets in the centre, surrounded by radiating longer white ray florets; heads borne in long-stalked clusters.
FLOWERING TIME  April–October.
DISTRIBUTION  Widespread across most of Europe in suitable habitats.
HABITAT  Favours disturbed ground, cultivated soil, tracks and waste places. Often forms extensive carpets in suitable locations.

## Feverfew
*Tanacetum parthenium*

SIZE AND DESCRIPTION  Up to 50 cm tall. An upright perennial that is downy and aromatic. Leaves are yellowish-green and pinnately divided; lower ones long-stalked, upper ones unstalked. Flower heads are daisy-like and 1–2 cm across, comprising yellow central disc florets surrounded by radiating white ray florets.

FLOWERING TIME  July–September.

DISTRIBUTION  Native to south-east Europe. Widespread across much of the rest of Europe except far north.

HABITAT  Favours disturbed ground, roadsides and walls.

## Colt's-foot
*Tussilago farfara*

SIZE AND DESCRIPTION  Up to 15 cm tall. A perennial, best known for its flower spikes, which appear in early spring. Leaves are large and round, with shallow lobes and teeth around the margin. Flower heads are 15–35 mm across and comprise yellow central disc florets and paler yellow ray florets; flowers are solitary and borne on stems with purple scales.

FLOWERING TIME  February–April.

DISTRIBUTION  Widespread across most of Europe.

HABITAT  Bare and often disturbed ground, usually on damp clayey soils.

### Butterbur

*Petasites hybridus*

SIZE AND DESCRIPTION  Up to 50 cm tall. An impressive perennial herb with a creeping rootstock; flowers appear first before leaves emerge. Leaves are up to 1 m across and heart-shaped with blunt teeth around the margin; green above and downy grey below. Flower heads are dense and pinkish-lilac; borne in stout spikes of up to 130 heads on stems with purple scales. Male flowers larger than females and borne on separate plants.

FLOWERING TIME  March–May.

DISTRIBUTION  Widespread across much of Europe although least common in the south and absent from the far north.

HABITAT  Favours damp ground in waterside habitats.

### Common fleabane
*Pulicaria dysenterica*

SIZE AND DESCRIPTION  Up to 60 cm tall. A branched and woolly perennial that is distinctive and showy only when in flower. Leaves are oblong-lanceolate with wavy margins; green above but greyish below. Flower heads 15–30 mm across with orange-yellow central disc florets and bright yellow outer ray floret; heads borne in open clusters. Leaves have insecticidal properties.
FLOWERING TIME  July–September.
DISTRIBUTION  Widespread across western, central and southern Europe.
HABITAT  Favours damp ground in meadows, marshes and ditches.

### Greater burdock
*Arctium lappa*

SIZE AND DESCRIPTION  Up to 1 m tall. A downy and branched perennial that is robust and upright in habit. Leaves are alternate, heart-shaped at the base and large. Flower heads are 3–4 cm across, egg-shaped and short-stalked, comprising dense purple disc florets and bracts with hooked spiny tips. In seed, these catch in animal fur to assist dispersal.
FLOWERING TIME  July–September.
DISTRIBUTION  Widespread throughout most of Europe except the far north.
HABITAT  Favours dry grassy places, roadside verges and open woodland.

## Spear thistle
*Cirsium vulgare*
SIZE AND DESCRIPTION

Up to 3 m tall. A branched and upright biennial with stems that are cottony, winged and armed with sharp spines between the leaves. Leaves are pinnately lobed and spiny; often downy beneath. Flower heads are 2–4 cm across and comprise purple florets arising from a ball of spiny bracts. Often considered as a persistent weed.

FLOWERING TIME July–September.

DISTRIBUTION Widespread throughout most of Europe.

HABITAT Favours disturbed ground, often common on wasteland and tracks.

## Meadow thistle
*Cirsium dissectum*

SIZE AND DESCRIPTION  Up to 80 cm tall. An upright perennial with a creeping rootstock and stems that are ridged, downy and unwinged. Leaves are oval, toothed and green and hairy above but white cottony below. Flower heads are 20–25 mm across and comprise reddish-purple florets arising from a ball of dark bracts; solitary and borne on long, spineless stalks.
FLOWERING TIME  June–August.
DISTRIBUTION  Widespread in western Europe only, but local and declining.
HABITAT  Restricted to damp peaty soils in bogs and meadows.

## Chicory
*Cichorium intybus*

SIZE AND DESCRIPTION  Up to 1 m tall. An upright and branched perennial with grooved stems; plant can be hairy or hairless. Easily overlooked when flowers are not open. Lower leaves are stalked and lobed while upper ones are narrow and clasping. Flower heads are 2–3 cm across and sky blue; open only on sunny mornings.
FLOWERING TIME  July–October.
DISTRIBUTION  Widespread throughout much of Europe in suitable habitats.
HABITAT  Favours dry grassy places and often locally common on roadside verges.

### Common knapweed
*Centaurea nigra*

SIZE AND DESCRIPTION  Up to 1 m tall. An upright perennial that is roughly hairy and has grooved stems that branch towards the top. The leaves are narrow and those near the base of the plant are slightly lobed. Flower heads are 2–4 cm across and comprise purple florets arising from a ball of brown bracts.

FLOWERING TIME June–September.

DISTRIBUTION  Widespread across central and western Europe as far north as southern Scandinavia; essentially absent from Mediterranean region.

HABITAT  Favours all sorts of grassy places including meadows and roadside verges.

## Lesser hawkbit
*Leontodon saxatilis*
SIZE AND DESCRIPTION Up to 40 cm tall. An unbranched perennial herb with stems that are hairless above but bristly below. Leaves are pinnately lobed with wavy-toothed margins. Flower heads are 20–25 mm across with yellow florets; flowers are solitary and borne on unbranched and leafless stalks. Seeds are wind-dispersed.
FLOWERING TIME June–October.
DISTRIBUTION Widespread throughout much of western southern and central Europe.
HABITAT Favours dry grassy habitats, usually on chalky or sandy soils.

## Smooth hawk's-beard
*Crepis capillaris*
SIZE AND DESCRIPTION Up to 1 m tall. An upright and hairless annual or biennial that is much-branched from the base. Leaves are usually hairless and pinnately divided into triangular lobes. Flower heads are 10–15 mm across and comprise yellow florets, the outer ones of which are often tinged red; borne in loose clusters.
FLOWERING TIME June–November.
DISTRIBUTION Widespread in western, central and southern Europe.
HABITAT Grassy and wasteland, including meadows and verges.

### Common hawkweed
*Hieracium vulgatum*

SIZE AND DESCRIPTION  Up to 80 cm tall. An upright perennial with stems that are usually leafy and yield a milky sap when broken. Basal leaves are ovate stalked and toothed; arranged as a rosette; stem leaves are unstalked. Flower heads are 2–3 cm across and comprise yellow florets; borne in groups of up to 20 heads.

FLOWERING TIME  July–September.

DISTRIBUTION  Widespread in western and central Europe but scarce or absent elsewhere.

HABITAT  Favours a variety of habitats from woods and banks to heaths and shady hedgerows.

## Honeysuckle
*Lonicera periclymenum*

SIZE AND DESCRIPTION  Up to 6 m long. A vigorous, deciduous and woody climber that often twines through the branches of trees and shrubs to assist its progress. Leaves are oblong to elliptical, dark green above but greyish-green below; borne in opposite pairs. Flowers are 35–55 mm long and comprise a creamy white tube; borne on long-stalked terminal heads. Flowers are sweet-scented. Fruits are red berries.

FLOWERING TIME  June–October.

DISTRIBUTION  Widespread in western, central and southern Europe.

HABITAT  Favours woodlands and hedgerows.

## Arrowhead
*Sagittaria sagittifolia*
SIZE AND DESCRIPTION  Up to 90 cm tall. An upright and hairless aquatic perennial. Aerial leaves are shaped like arrowheads and borne on long upright stalks. Plant also has floating and submerged leaves. Flowers are 15–20 mm across and comprise three white petals, each with a purple spot at the base; borne in whorls.
FLOWERING TIME  July–August.
DISTRIBUTION  Widespread in most of Europe except the far north and the Mediterranean region.
HABITAT  Still or slow-moving waters.

## Bluebell
*Hyacinthoides non-scripta*
SIZE AND DESCRIPTION  Up to 50 cm tall. A bulbous perennial. Leaves are long, narrow and bright green; up to 30 cm long with three to six arising from base of plant. Flowers are 14–20 mm long, bluish-purple and bell-shaped, comprise six segments that are fused at the base.
FLOWERING TIME  April–June.
DISTRIBUTION  Widespread in western Europe; and parts of central Europe.
HABITAT  Favours open woodland, often where coppicing management has taken place; also in hedgerows and on sea cliffs. Forms extensive carpets in suitable locations.

## Ramsons
*Allium ursinum*

SIZE AND DESCRIPTION  Up
to 50 cm tall. A distinctive
and upright bulbous
perennial that smells strongly
of garlic when bruised. Stem is
sharply-angled. Each bulb
produces two bright green leaves
that are up to 25 cm long, stalked and
elongate ovate. Flowers are up to 2 cm
across and comprise six white segments;
borne in long-stalked, flat-topped umbels
of up to 25 flowers, up to 6 cm across.
FLOWERING TIME  April–June.
DISTRIBUTION  Widespread across most of
Europe except the Mediterranean region
and the north-east.
HABITAT  Favours woodland, usually on
damp or calcareous soils. Often locally
abundant and carpet-forming.

## Herb-Paris
*Paris quadrifolia*

SIZE AND DESCRIPTION Up to 40 cm tall. A distinctive and unusual upright perennial with a creeping rootstock. Upright stems carry a single whorl of unstalked oval to diamond-shaped leaves that are 5–16 cm long and conspicuously veined. Flower is solitary, borne on a long stalk and comprises four to six green sepals and four or more narrow petals topped by a purple ovary and yellow stamens.

FLOWERING TIME May–July.

DISTRIBUTION Widespread across most of Europe except the Mediterranean.

HABITAT Damp woods, calcareous soils.

## Yellow flag
*Iris pseudacorus*

SIZE AND DESCRIPTION Up to 1.2 m tall. A striking perennial with a large, fleshy rhizome. Leaves are sword-shaped, bluish-green and up to 1 m long. Stems are slightly flattened. Flowers are up to 10 cm across, deep yellow, and comprise six segments, the three outer being broad and long; flowers borne in groups of two or three.

FLOWERING TIME June–July.

DISTRIBUTION Widespread across most of Europe.

HABITAT Damp soils. River and pond margins and water meadows.

## Lords-and-ladies
*Arum maculatum*
SIZE AND DESCRIPTION
Up to 25 cm tall. An
upright and hairless perennial. Leaves are
arrowhead-shaped, long-stalked and shiny green but
sometimes purple-spotted; appear in the early spring
before flowers. Flowers are borne on a spike, male flowers
above female ones, but the whole hidden at base of yellow-
green spathe and below purple-brown cylindrical spadix.
Ripe berries are bright red and appear in autumn.
FLOWERING TIME April–May.
DISTRIBUTION Widespread in western, central and southern Europe.
HABITAT Favours woodland and shady hedgerows, usually on
damp soils.

## Common spotted-orchid
*Dactylorhiza fuchsii*

SIZE AND DESCRIPTION Up to 65 cm tall. An upright perennial. Has five to twelve leaves that are shiny green and dark-spotted; upper ones are shorter and narrower than lower ones. Flowers are 12–18 mm across and pinkish-purple; the lower three-lobed lip is marked with dark spots and lines. Flowers are borne in tall, dense spikes.
FLOWERING TIME June–August.
DISTRIBUTION Widespread across most of Europe except southern regions.
HABITAT Favours grassy habitats, usually on chalky or neutral soils. Often locally abundant.

## Pyramidal orchid
*Anacamptis pyramidalis*

SIZE AND DESCRIPTION Up to 60 cm tall. An upright perennial. Leaves are lanceolate and grey-green; usually carried upright and partly sheathe the flowering stem. Flowers are 5–10 mm across, deep pink and have a three-lobed lip and a long spur; borne in dense heads that are conical or domed.
FLOWERING TIME June–August.
DISTRIBUTION Widespread across much of central, western and southern Europe, absent from most of the north.
HABITAT Favours dry, grassy habitats, usually on calcareous soils. Often locally abundant.

## Bee orchid
*Ophrys apifera*
SIZE AND DESCRIPTION  Up to 50 cm tall.
An extremely distinctive perennial.
Basal leaves are ovate-lanceolate and
form a rosette; stem leaves are
narrower ovate. Flowers are 12–25 mm
across and comprise three pink
segments, two narrow green ones and
a maroon and furry lower segment
that is expanded to form a lip; yellow
markings on the lip add to its fanciful
resemblance to a bumblebee. Flowers
borne in spikes of up to eight.
FLOWERING TIME  June–July.
DISTRIBUTION  Widespread across
much of Europe.
HABITAT  Favours dry grassland,
usually on chalky soils.

# Addresses

Emorsgate Seeds
Limes Farm
Tilney All Saints
Kings Lynn PE34 4RT
Tel 01553 829028
Fax 01553 829803

Landlife Wildflowers Ltd
National Wildflower Centre
Court Hey Park
Liverpool L16 3NA
Tel 0151 737 1819
Fax 0151 737 1820
E-mail info@wildflower.org.uk
Website www.wildflower.org.uk

Plantlife
21 Elizabeth Street
London SW1W 9RP
Tel 020 7808 0100
Fax 020 7730 8377
E-mail enquiries@plantlife.org.uk
Website www.plantlife.org.uk

Wild Flower Society
82a High Street
Sawston
Cambridge CB2 4HJ
Tel 01223 830665
E-mail wfs@grantais.demon.co.uk
Website www.rbge.org.uk/data/wfsoc

The Wildlife Trusts
The Kiln
Waterside
Mather Road
Newark
Nottinghamshire NG24 1WT
Tel 0870 036 7711
Fax 0870 036 0101
E-mail info@wildlife-trusts.cix.co.uk
Website www.wildlifetrusts.org

Wildlife Watch
(Contact details as above)
E-mail watch@wildlife-trusts.cix.co.uk

# Suggested reading

Fitter, Richard, Fitter, Alistair &
Blamey, Marjorie
*The Wild Flowers of Britain and
Northern Europe*
Collins, 1996

Garrard, Ian, and Streeter, David
*The Wild Flowers of the British Isles*
Macmillan, 1983

Gibbons, Bob, & Brough, Peter
*The Hamlyn Photographic Guide to the Wild
Flowers of Britain & Northern Europe*
Hamlyn, 1992

Grey-Wilson, Christopher
*Wild Flowers of Britain and
Northwest Europe*
Dorling Kindersley, 1994

Mabey, Richard
*Flora Britannica*
Sinclair Stevenson, 1996

Rackham, Oliver
*The Illustrated History of the Countryside*
Weidenfield & Nicholson, 1994

Rose, Francis
*The Wild Flower Key*
Warne, 1981

# Index